Introd.

This book was written during the Coronavirus lockdown period because the author was bored and wanted something to do. The result is a set of questions that are designed to stretch your mind.

Some of the questions are simple, light-hearted silliness. Others pose philosophical wonderings and moral dilemmas. Others explore matters of taste and personal preference.

Be as pedantic as you like. Look for loopholes. Take things literally or figuratively. It doesn't matter. Just enjoy the debate.

To aid enquiry, some things to consider are listed underneath each question.

Some weird and wonderful situations are set out in these pages. It is not recommended that you endanger yourself, or anyone else, in attempting to recreate or act out any of the situations mentioned.

WWYR?

Be able to fly for five minutes per day?

OR

Be able to hold your breath for two hours per day?

Things to Consider

Would you use your ability to avoid the traffic on your way to work? Or go for an evening pleasure flight to unwind after the day is done?

Perhaps you will spend your evenings walking along the seabed looking for treasure.

WWYR?

Never have to eat again?

OR

Have free food in restaurants for the rest of your life?

Things to Consider

You are going to save lots of money and never again have indigestion. You will also have lots more free time since you won't be food shopping or sitting down to eat. But will you miss meals with friends and family? Will you miss talking about flavours and textures?

Would you eat out all of the time? Would this make you lazy and cause you to eat more than you should? Will this choice increase your intake of unhealthy foods?

WWYR?

Never again travel beyond ten miles of your current home?

OR

Move to the other side of the world and never travel more than 50 miles from your new home?

Things to Consider

Are you happy to stay close to family and friends? Or do you crave to see farther afield? Will you spend the rest of your life wondering what's out there?

Could you take a chance and risk starting a completely new life without looking back? Are you going to be homesick? Will you make do with your family and friends coming to visit you a few times per year?

WWYR?

Have the ability to travel forward in time five minutes once per day?

OR

Have the ability to travel back in time five minutes once per day?

Things to Consider

Do you want to know what someone is going to say before they say it? Or maybe you would frequent casinos and try to win a fortune whilst trying not to raise suspicion?

Do you want the ability to fix a mistake once each day? Are you prone to making mistakes or unintentionally offending people? Would it increase your confidence to know that your wrong moves can be erased?

WWYR?

Be able to hear other people's private thoughts? **OR** Be able to see through other people's eyes?

Things to Consider

Do you really want to know what people think of you? Would you become an ace negotiator who is always one step ahead of the other party?

You could use your powers to help authorities find criminals. Or would you spend an unhealthy amount of time spying and being voyeuristic?

WWYR?

Have a dog's
sense of smell?   **OR**   Have the vision of
                                   a hawk?

Things to Consider

Would you like to
be able to smell
fear? Won't
people laugh at
you because your
nose is always
twitching and you
have a tendency
to want to
navigate by
scent?

What would you
do with
high-resolution
images from a
distance? Perhaps
you would
become the
ultimate search
and rescue
volunteer who
flies over
mountains in a
helicopter
surveying every
detail below. Do
you want to be a
hero?

WWYR?

Have the ability to spin silk like a spider?

OR

Have the ability to administer fatal venom with a bite?

Things to Consider

You could abseil any time that you like or swing yourself around your nearest city. Would your ability become a curse in that you are constantly bothered by comic book fans who want you to do tricks for them?

How much confidence would you have if you never had to fear an enemy again? Would you trust yourself not to snap and murder innocent people who have merely annoyed you?

WWYR?

Be able to make yourself invisible? **OR** Be able to shapeshift?

Things to Consider

Do you like the thought of walking around in places that you aren't supposed to be in? No one will see you but what about thermal imaging cameras? Would you be worried that your body heat is visible? Will people think that you are a predator and shoot at you?

You can transform into any physical object. So would you turn yourself into a piece of furniture in a boardroom and listen in on private meetings? Would this hobby become addictive and take up too much of your time?

WWYR?

| Eat a live chicken? | **OR** | Be locked in a room with a crocodile for 12 hours? |

Things to Consider

Everything has to go: feathers, beak, feet, the lot. No cooking is allowed. Have you got the patience, mental strength and stomach to complete the job?

You're going to have to kill it, or it will certainly kill and eat you. They're famously good at it. Can you survive?

WWYR?

Have an extra arm? **OR** Have an extra leg?

Things to Consider

With all of this extra dexterity would you become the world's greatest juggler or train to become the most-skilled surgeon ever to live? Would buying clothes be an issue?

With some training would you become a running ace or a champion kick-boxer? Would you worry that people would make fun of you behind your back? Or would the celebrity status that you achieve outway any anxieties that you have?

WWYR?

Have a pouch like a kangaroo? **OR** Have the long neck of a giraffe?

Things to Consider

Surely this would be convenient. No need to carry a bag around with you anymore, you have one built into your body. But will it be sore and uncomfortable to clean? Would you put a vacuum cleaner in there to suck up dust and lint?

Fancy the idea of towering over everyone? You will certainly turn heads, but maybe you like to stand out. Are people going to think of you as a nuisance in the cinema or theatre?

WWYR?

Have spines like a hedgehog? **OR** Have a shell like a tortoise?

Things to Consider

Do you like the idea of being able to roll up into a ball and protect yourself from attackers? Is it going to be inconvenient to have spines on your back? Or, is this preferable to wearing clothes?

Are you a nervous person? Would you like to be able to retreat into your shell and wait for passing inconveniences to go away?

WWYR?

Be reincarnated as a dog? **OR** Be reincarnated as a cat?

Things to Consider

Dogs are primarily concerned with eating and messing around. Does that sound like the sort of lifestyle you could become accustomed to? Or are dogs too loyal? Is this sometimes to their detriment?

Would you like to be super agile and be able to jump six times your own height? Do you want to spend the vast majority of the day doing whatever you please and sleeping? Or do you think that cats are viewed as selfish, self-centred bird murderers? Maybe you don't care.

WWYR?

Die by walking into the sea and drowning?

OR

Die by being burned at the stake?

Things to Consider

Some say that having your lungs fill with water, so that you slowly slip away, is a peaceful way to go. But would you have the mental fortitude and bravery to take that walk?

At least you aren't making any decisions in this situation, it is being done <u>TO</u> you. But can you cope with having your skin boil and your eyes pop? You are going to be dead anyway, so does it matter?

WWYR?

Execute a criminal   **OR**   Execute a criminal
by lethal injection?   by electric chair?

Things to Consider

Could you depress the syringe and see someone's life slip away?

Can you press the button and watch someone buzz as electrical current courses through their body?

WWYR?

Give up drinking tea for the rest of your life? **OR** Give up drinking coffee for the rest of your life?

Things to Consider

Do you enjoy a cup of tea in the evening to help you unwind after work? How much are you going to miss this simple pleasure?

Do you need a hit of caffeine in the morning to wake you up? Is coffee essential fuel for you throughout the day? If so, is it unthinkable to have to give it up?

WWYR?

For the rest of your life, only be awake for one hour per day?

OR

For the rest of your life, only sleep for one hour per day?

Things to Consider

Can you cram everything you want to do in a day into 60 minutes? Would this make you highly efficient? What can you do in an hour to make enough money to live on?

Would you get bored being awake for 23 hours each day? Or would you enjoy having more time to do stuff? Will you suffer psychological side effects if your mind doesn't get enough down time?

WWYR?

For the rest of your life have sound but no sight.

OR

For the rest of your life have sight but no sound?

Things to Consider

At least you will always be able to hear your favourite music and chat to your friends and family. But are you going to miss seeing the world around you?

Are images your biggest stimulus? Do you enjoy seeing people, landscapes and the sunset? Can you really give up listening to the sound of the ocean just so that you can see it?

18

WWYR?

Never have
internet access
again?

OR

Never see your
friends again in
person?

Things to Consider

Would you get
used to not having
online banking? Do
you think you
would have more
free time if you
weren't online so
much? Or is this
option
inconceivable as
you would
become too
detached and
isolated from the
online world?

You can still see
your friends
online and have
video chats. Is
that good enough
or would you miss
being in their
presence?

WWYR?

Have extendable arms?   **OR**   Have extendable legs?

Things to Consider

Would you find it convenient to be able to reach up and retrieve objects that are usually out of reach? Perhaps you would take up a sport in which extendable arms are an advantage. Cricket? Baseball? Basketball? Would you be scared of punching people by mistake?

Would it make you feel safe to know that you can activate your special legs and flee unwelcome situations at high speed? Can you cope with the attention that your ability is going to draw? Will people call you cruel names?

WWYR?

Never be allowed to brush your teeth again?

OR

Never be allowed to wash your body again?

Things to Consider

If you choose this option it is a matter of time before your teeth fall out? How are you going to chew your food?

Would you get used to being greasy and smelly? Some say that if you don't wash for long enough then you stop needing to.

WWYR?

Be able to see in the dark? **OR** Have magnetic feet?

Things to Consider

Will you feel safer knowing that no one can sneak up on you in the dark? Would you become a sought-after sentry or bodyguard? Is your body clock going to suffer because you're tempted to stay up all night watching what's going on?

On the plus side, you will look cool when you do tricks like walking up a steel building or running upside down underneath a bridge. But, on the downside, will you have to avoid certain situations that involve metal such as getting in and out of cars?

WWYR?

Know the date of
your death ten
years in advance?   **OR**   Know the date of
your death ten
days in advance?

Things to Consider

Is a decade the
perfect amount
of time to wind
your life down
yet still plan how
to best use your
remaining time?
Or do you see
this as a
torturous, slow
decline?

Is it better to not
know too far in
advance? Would
you go out with a
bang and have the
best ten days of
your life? Or is
this insufficient
time to do all of
the things you
want to do and
say all of your
goodbyes?

WWYR?

Always know everything there is to know?

OR

Know what you know now but never learn anything new for the rest of your life?

Things to Consider

Would it be reassuring to you to know that you are one step ahead of everyone because you automatically have access to all knowledge? Or can you know too much? Will all of this information be a burden?

Are you sure you know enough now to get you through to the end of your life? Will you always be wondering what else has happened in the world since you switched off your learning?

WWYR?

Have your current hairstyle forever?

OR

Have a different hairstyle every month for the rest of your life?

Things to Consider

Do you want to play it safe and stick with what you've got? It's likely that no one will ever notice or mention it. But will you become bored and start daydreaming about all of the styles that you could have tried out?

Does this sound exciting to you? Do you like being daring and creative? How quickly would you run out of ideas though? Can you come up with 12 different styles each year?

WWYR?

Float like a
butterfly?   **OR**   Sting like a bee?

Things to Consider

Do you want to
be viewed as
elegant, delicate
and graceful? Or,
in having this sort
of disposition,
would you worry
that people will
think of you as
weak and
vulnerable?

Do you prefer to
be considered a
fierce, acerbic,
prickly 'one to
watch'? In
choosing this
option are you
worried that
people will be
afraid of you?
Or is that what
you want?

WWYR?

Be an Olympic
gold medallist?

OR

Win a Nobel
Peace Prize?

Things to Consider

Do you want to
be remembered
for sporting
prowess? Is this
what Man has
been aiming at
since the first
games in 776BC?
Or do you think
of sport as futile
and worthless?

Do you want the
world to
remember you
for the work
you did to foster
fraternity
between nations
and reduce
conflict? Is this
the only thing that
really matters?
Or is the pursuit
of peace
pointless given
humanity's
self-destructive
tendencies?

27

WWYR?

Be able to change the natural colour of your eyes at will?

OR

Be able to change the natural colour of your hair at will?

Things to Consider

If you have blue eyes, would you prefer to have brown? Maybe you like green eyes. Or something completely different like pink or purple? Will this make you stand out from the crowd or make you look like a weirdo?

Do you spend a lot of money dying your hair? Would this option be more convenient? Perhaps you want to change your hair to match your outfit. If you can change your hair colour at any point, will you lose loads of time each day trying new colours?

WWYR?

Have a baseball thrown at your head from a distance of 20m?

OR

Have a dart thrown at your chest from a distance of 3m?

Things to Consider

Baseballs are very hard but at least they are blunt. The impact is going to hurt and you will be bruised. Is this experience going to be preferable to the dart?

3m is a relatively short distance so the impact will be lower than if the dart was dropped on you from a great height. But the tip of the dart is sharp so all of its energy is focussed into a small surface area. It will pierce your skin. But how badly?

WWYR?

Overnight, become a world-class pianist?

OR

Wake up tomorrow with a singing voice that everyone loves?

Things to Consider

Do you want to wake up tomorrow and be able to run your fingers over those keys like a boss? On the downside, you can only play when there's a piano nearby. But you can sing anywhere.

Would you like to be the surprise hit at every party or gathering you attend? Can you picture yourself brightening up every situation with your silky voice? Would you worry that people only want you around for your voice and forget about who you are?

WWYR?

Torture a traitor to make them talk by using thumbscrews?

OR

Torture a traitor to make them talk through the use of cigarette burns?

Things to Consider

The pain is constant and only gets worse as you gradually tighten the screw to encourage compliance. Do you have the mental strength to watch someone endure ever-increasing discomfort?

The burns will deliver short, sharp bursts of intense pain. Can you cope with the smell of burning flesh and the look of fear on the traitor's face?

WWYR?

Instead of hands, have Captain Hook attachments?

OR

Have scissors instead of fingers?

Things to Consider

What can you do with hooks? Probably more than you think. You can pick things up, eat certain foods and even scratch your head. But are there going to be certain situations in which you wish you had the scissor fingers?

Do you want to be the go-to person for cutting things? Or be an ace hair stylist? Would you worry that you will hurt yourself, or someone else by accident when you are asleep?

WWYR?

Never eat cheese again?

OR

Never eat chips (fries in the USA) again?

Things to Consider

Is cheese one of life's greatest pleasures? Giving it up will improve your cholesterol levels, and general health, but can you stand the thought of never having cheese on toast again or never being able to order a cheese board in a restaurant?

Who doesn't like chips? How much would you miss them? If you give them up you can continue to eat cheese. But you'll never again be able to enjoy a steak and chips, a burger and chips or, the British classic, fish and chips.

WWYR?

Have a finger that can dispense water?

OR

Have an eye that can project a laser beam?

Things to Consider

There's got to be plenty of practical applications for a water-finger. As humans, water is something that we encounter and use a lot everyday. Would people always be hassling you for your water? Would this annoy you after a while?

Ok, so a laser-eye is a bit freaky and people will definitely be afraid of you and think you are weird. But there's a lot that can be done with lasers: cutting, drilling, welding, soldering and engraving, for example.

WWYR?

Be able to cast one spell per day? **OR** Be granted one wish per week?

Things to Consider

Casting a spell involves using your own power to achieve a result. Is this preferable to asking someone to grant you a wish? Is once a day too much? Will this ability make you too cocky?

Would having to ask for something from someone else make you more likely to consider carefully what you are asking for? If you have only one opportunity each week are you going to be frustrated or will you enjoy planning what to ask for?

WWYR?

Live in a forest for the rest of your life?

OR

Live in the jungle for the rest of your life?

Things to Consider

Do you fancy yourself as a survivalist? Is this going to be a walk in the park (pun intended) or are you too wedded to home comforts and modern appliances to make this a feasible option?

The jungle has got to contain everything you need to live on, right? But do you know how to make use of the resources? You might enjoy the hot, humid climate but what will the lurking presence of poisonous creatures do to your nerves?

WWYR?

Not be allowed to cut your nails for the rest of your life?

OR

Not be allowed to cut your hair for the rest of your life?

Things to Consider

Long nails might be cool for a while, but would they start to get in the way? They might be useful for hobbies like playing the guitar but will they be a nuisance when you're chopping vegetables or trying to button a shirt?

This is going to mean a lot of hair washing after a while. Is your hair curly or straight? Are you going to have to spend a lot of time combing? Maybe you love long hair. But will you miss being able to style it with fashionable cuts?

WWYR?

Be given a lifetime supply of bread and pasta?

OR

Be given a lifetime supply of fruit and vegetables?

Things to Consider

Is it all about carbs for you? Maybe you have a vegetable patch and a greenhouse at home and have no need for a supply of fruit and vegetables. If you're rubbish at working with flour then this might be the correct choice for you.

How much do you value the nutritional benefits of fresh fruit and vegetables? If you haven't got the means to grow them at home you might be spending a lot of money every month on these foods.

WWYR?

Never be allowed to eat red meat or chicken again?

OR

Never be allowed to eat fish, or any seafood, again?

Things to Consider

How much would you miss steaks and chicken nuggets? Or do you think eating meat is unhealthy, or even immoral, and welcome the opportunity to become vegetarian?

No more fish and chips. No more prawns , crab or lobster. Can you really give up these foods? Maybe you don't like seafood anyway and so will find this choice an easy one to make.

WWYR?

Have the fingers of one hand each be able to write in a different colour like pens?

OR

Have scissors instead of two fingers on your non-dominant hand?

Things to Consider

Will you enjoy making wondrous creations with your multi-coloured hand? Or will you be forever having to clean accidental finger marks off your furniture?

That scissor-hand would surely be useful around the house or in the office. But will all of your household surfaces have scratches and dents on them from your metallic fingers?

WWYR?

Have an invisible eye on the back of your head? **OR** Be able to see around corners?

Things to Consider

Never have to look over your shoulder again. Do you want to be able to casually spy on what's going on behind you? Is it going to be awkward to sleep on? What if it becomes defective and needs a corrective lens? How's that going to work?

You would be an invaluable member of a SWAT team or a useful lookout for a gang of thieves. Will you miss the feeling of surprise when you turn a corner and see something amazing or unexpected?

WWYR?

Have the running speed of a cheetah?

OR

Have the climbing agility of a lion?

Things to Consider

Cheetahs can go from 0-70mph in about four seconds. Would you enjoy out-sprinting cars for fun? Would you need to be careful with your body though? Too much running may damage your knees and joints.

Lions can pull themselves up trees with their claws. This is pretty impressive but how useful is it to be able to climb trees quickly? Is there much call for that in your day-to-day life?

WWYR?

In your day-to-day life have a VAR function to adjudicate disputes?

OR

Have a Hawkeye function to ensure precision in your day-to-day life?

Things to Consider

Do you really want independent scrutiny of your actions? This might be a bit intrusive and make you feel like you are not in charge of your own life. On the other hand, it might help you to live a more virtuous existence.

Does precision appeal to you? Would this function help with tasks such as parking a car? If Hawkeye started to become addictive would you start using it for frivolous pursuits like tracking the flight path of birds in the sky?

43

WWYR?

Have expandable memory so you can plug a flash drive into your mind?

OR

Have your memory erased every ten years?

Things to Consider

Are you struggling for memory space? Do you forget too many things? Want to never forget? Or is it healthy that some things are naturally forgotten and replaced with new things? Is it necessary to block out certain memories and move on?

Do you have too many bad memories? Want to reset and reboot once a decade? Or will you miss your memories? What will it feel like to look at pictures from your childhood and have no recollection of the times they represent?

WWYR?

For the rest of
your life be given   **OR**   stressed for the
30% extra   Be 30% less
intelligence?   rest of your life?

Things to Consider

Do you feel that
life would be
easier if you
were sharper?
Do you want to
feel that you
have the edge
over the rest of
the room? If you
can see the world
more clearly will
you be more or
less happy in it?

How much does
stress impede
your day-to-day
performance?
Would it feel
better to be able
to cruise through
the day without a
care? Or is it
stress that keeps
you focussed and
motivated?

WWYR?

Have spaghetti instead of hair? **OR** Be able to cry wine instead of tears?

Things to Consider

Would this look cool and quirky or weird and unattractive? Would your hair be a useful source of carbohydrate? Would it feel odd to be eating your own hair with bolognese or would this feel satisfying?

How much wine could you realistically harvest? It might take many tears to produce a useful volume of liquid. However, if you are upset and crying your eyes out at least you will have a glass of vino at the end to cheer you up.

WWYR?

Be able to instantly calculate any mathematical equation?

OR

Know every word of every language in the world?

Things to Consider

Would you use your skills to make money from gambling? Or would you apply your ability to furthering mathematical enquiry? Would you start to see the world as just numbers, and would this dull your appreciation of aesthetic beauty?

How much could you earn as the World's greatest linguist? Would you enjoy travelling the world and seeing the shock on other people's faces as you effortlessly converse in an obscure dialect? Or would people think you were a freak?

WWYR?

Be able to hear through the ears of another person of your choice?

OR

Be able to see through the eyes of another person of your choice?

Things to Consider

How would you use your eavesdropping powers? Would it be difficult to choose who the other person is (you can only have one)? Would you feel like you were compromising a moral code in using espionage for your advantage?

What would you spy on through another person's eyes? Perhaps you want to keep track of a partner or child to make sure they are safe. Although your intentions are good, is this an invasion of their privacy?

WWYR?

Be able to plant thoughts in other people's minds?

OR

Be able to plant images in other people's minds?

Things to Consider

Would you use your powers to make someone like you? Perhaps you would change their thoughts to pull them out of a low point or depression. Even if your motivations are healthy, is it ok to interfere with someone's thoughts?

In conversation, do you often find yourself saying 'do you know what I mean?' Would it be convenient to simply transfer a mental image to the other party? Do you trust yourself to only use your powers for good?

WWYR?

Be chosen to be part of a group that will populate a new planet next week?

OR

Go back in time and be one of the first settlers of a newly discovered landmass on the earth?

Things to Consider

Would you take a big risk but be considered a modern hero for striding into the unknown future to benefit mankind? What if it goes wrong and your spacecraft crashes? Are you still a hero for taking a chance? Was it worth it?

Wouldn't it be fascinating to see how humans from a previous era lived? Or would it be brutal and terrifying? Is this choice preferable to flying into space with a group of interplanetary settlers?

WWYR?

Have a lump sum inheritance that is equal to 30 times your current annual income (but you can't have it until you are 75)?

OR

Have a lump sum that is equal to twice your annual earnings deposited into your bank account tomorrow?

Things to Consider

Can you wait? How close are you to 75? What's your life expectancy? Will you become complacent in your current day-to-day life because you know the big payday is coming?

What would you do tomorrow? Book a holiday? Buy a shiny, fast, new car? Maybe you would invest the money or give it to charity. As you get older would you regret having not waited for the larger amount?

WWYR?

Have immunity to
all viruses?

OR

Be unable to be
physically
damaged?

Things to Consider

Would you feel
reassured to
never have to
worry about
social distancing
concerns again?
Would you feel
under pressure
to be the subject
of a scientific
study to
understand your
super-immunity?
Would you be
constantly probed
and tested?

Jump off a cliff
for a laugh? Let
yourself be run
over by a truck
as a party trick?
The possibilities
are endless. But
would you worry
that you are
setting a bad
example? Are
others going to
hurt themselves
by trying to be
like you?

WWYR?

Acquire the skills of a master magician?

OR

Acquire the skills of a master gymnast?

Things to Consider

Make money and entertain people with vanishing skills and exquisite sleight of hand? Perhaps you will become a con artist and make millions? Which path would you take? Good or evil?

What could you get up to with the finely-tuned body of a gymnast? Would you become a daring burglar who can glide over and around physical barriers? Or would you train to attempt a gold-medal-winning Olympic performance? Will your knees and joints suffer?

WWYR?

Never be allowed to drink alcoholic drinks again?

OR

Never be allowed to drink fizzy drinks again?

Things to Consider

How much would you miss the relief that booze brings at the end of the day? Or would you embrace the opportunity to make a positive change to your health and possibly extend your life expectancy?

Remember that beer and champagne are fizzy (you can't have anything that is carbonated). Is this a small enough luxury to give up without noticing? Or will you miss the effervescent thrill of bubbles in your mouth?

WWYR?

Not be allowed to use your hands to eat?

OR

Not be allowed to use your hands to drink?

Things to Consider

Could you really chow down like a dog? Is it undignified to eat with your face in a bowl of food? Or would you get used to it and find it to be a refreshing change?

Would you lap up your fluids like a cat? Or pick up your glass with your mouth? Are you worried about lots of spillages and broken glasses? Would you use plastic tumblers instead of glass vessels?

WWYR?

Give up your ability to read printed text ever again?

OR

Give up your ability to hear music ever again?

Things to Consider

Imagine walking around a shop and not being able to read any of the prices. Will this damage your confidence? Or do you consider reading words to be an inconvenience? These days computers can do it all for us anyway, right?

Would life be unbearably boring without music? Would you feel left out since everyone else can enjoy sounds that you can't? Or maybe you would welcome the peace and quiet.

WWYR?

Have to sleep in a ventilated coffin six feet under the ground in a cemetery for one week?

OR

Sleep naked in a glass box in the centre of your nearest town for one week?

Things to Consider

Have you got the mental strength to deal with the dark, the cold and being surrounded by decaying cadavers? Or will this give you a quiet, contemplative opportunity to arrange your thoughts?

Are you bashful? Could you really have yourself on show for all to see? Maybe you are a natural exhibitionist and would look forward to bedtime in the glass box.

WWYR?

Give up watching television (both digital and analogue) for the rest of your life?

OR

Never go to another bar, eatery, cinema or live concert again?

Things to Consider

Do you really need TV? Could you get by with just the internet for entertainment? Or would you miss talking about your favourite shows with your family, friends and colleagues?

You would save money but would you miss the social interaction too much to give it up? Avoiding bars will potentially bring you health benefits but is there something special about live concerts that makes you feel alive?

WWYR?

Have wheels at the end of your legs instead of feet?

OR

Have springs on the end of your legs instead of feet?

Things to Consider

You could give your legs a rest as you cruise along. This will be great going down hills or gliding along level surfaces. But what about going uphill? Will you have to have some sort of braking mechanism installed?

What could you spring up to reach? Will onlookers be jealous of you or find your appearance and motion comical? Do you care?

WWYR?

Shoot a random civilian from a rooftop?

OR

Shoot a family's pet dog in front of them?

Things to Consider

Can you live with the guilt of ending a person's life for no reason? Or does it not really matter because we're all going to die anyway? Maybe the person was in pain and distress. Maybe your act was an inadvertent kindness. Maybe, maybe not.

This might be a difficult thing to do. Is it more difficult because you have an audience? Or, is this easy because it's only a dog and dogs aren't people so who cares? What about the effect on the family? Does that matter?

WWYR?

Have razor blades instead of finger nails?   **OR**   Have metal hooks instead of toes?

Things to Consider

These would be both handy and dangerous. But in what ratio? Will the convenience of being able to cut and slice things easily be outweighed by the potential harm that you could do to yourself by accident?

Gain extra traction? Have a secret, unexpected defence mechanism? Are you going to have to give up wearing socks or keep mending all of the holes in them?

WWYR?

Be put to death by hanging in public?

OR

Be put to death by strangulation in private?

Things to Consider

This would be a quick way to check out. But does the presence of an audience put you off? If you're going to die, does it matter who sees you?

With this method it could take a relatively-longer time to finish the job, depending on the skill of the executioner. But at least no one else will see you die.

WWYR?

Have scales
instead of skin?   **OR**   Have all bodily hair
moult four times
a year whether
you like it or not?

Things to Consider

Would this look
weird or cool?
Do scales require
less maintenance
than skin? What
products would
you use on your
scales to keep
them healthy?

You are going to
be bald four
times a year. Can
you deal with
that? Your head
will feel cool in
the summer heat,
but will you miss
having some head
insulation during
the winter?

WWYR?

Instead of your own thoughts have, instead, only internet search results?

OR

Never be able to search the internet again?

Things to Consider

You are giving up your own creative thoughts. Is that really a bad thing? Do you sometimes overthink things? Will this replacement search function make you more efficient? Are you still YOU in this situation?

Would you miss the reassurance that the internet brings you when you doubt yourself? Perhaps you like being your own person and see this option as a means of ensuring that you dance to your own beat.

WWYR?

Never have any new, original thoughts from midnight tonight?

OR

Lose all of your memories from midnight tonight and live with only the new information that you acquire from then on?

Things to Consider

Do you already have enough information to get you to the end of your life safely in a way that you can enjoy? Or, for the rest of your life will you feel that you are missing out by not having new ideas?

Do you want to wipe out the past and reboot? It might sound tempting but remember that you are going to have to learn EVERYTHING again, including language and toilet training.

WWYR?

Never be afraid again?   **OR**   Never again feel true love?

Things to Consider

How much could you achieve if you didn't have to overcome your fear? Is fear a healthy emotion that keeps you safe? Although you will be more confident, are you also putting yourself in greater danger?

Is true love really all that good? Or is it a bit too powerful and all-consuming? Maybe love is what makes you feel alive and the thought of living without it is unbearable.

WWYR?

Strangle a random civilian to death (no one ever suspects or discovers that you did it)?

OR

Donate 40% of your annual earnings to charity each year for the rest of your life?

Things to Consider

If no one knows you did it, and you are guaranteed to never be convicted, can you do it? At least, in choosing this option, you can keep all of your money and life is all about money. Right?

Are you going to have to make drastic changes to your lifestyle if you are 40% less wealthy each year? Is this even feasible? Or are you going to have to go through with the discreet murder?

WWYR?

Have Midas' touch of gold?

OR

Have Poseidon's ability to turn people and things to dust?

Things to Consider

If you could turn lots of things into gold would this quickly de-value the metal? Or would you be careful to conceal your new power, create gold in secrecy and slowly sell your wares to an unsuspecting market?

You would never have a problem dismantling anything ever again but people would be terrified of you. Are you going to have to be careful with your power? How many things do you have to turn to dust before you are locked up?

WWYR?

Be able to load software into your brain in order to choose between multiple, different versions of yourself to use in different situations?

OR

Upload a randomly-selected previous version of yourself (from one day in the past) that you have to stick with forever?

Things to Consider

You could choose the confident You to deal with pressurised situations. Or you could choose the assertive You for negotiations. Will you always be tinkering?

You might be assigned a version of yourself from a day when you felt great. But what if you are given a version of yourself from childhood, or from a day when you felt down?

69

WWYR?

Have feet for hands?   **OR**   Have hands for feet?

Things to Consider

Would you be able to run really fast on all fours? How useful is it to be able to kick with four limbs? Are you going to miss having manual dexterity for precise tasks such as writing and peeling bananas?

Doubling your dexterity is tempting. But will your feet-hands be sore and awkward to walk on?

WWYR?

With a saw, amputate one of your arms at the elbow?

OR

With a saw, amputate one of your legs at the knee?

Things to Consider

Your arms have hands at the ends of them. These are extremely useful devices. How much are you going to miss having two arms and two hands? At least the arm is thinner so the procedure and pain will be over more quickly.

This option is going to significantly restrict your mobility. And the surgery will take a longer time to perform. But with this option you still have the dexterity of two hands. Which is more important to you?

WWYR?

Have the ability to print counterfeit money without being caught?

OR

Have the ability to heal the sick?

Things to Consider

Extra cash would be useful, for sure. But can you live with yourself and the fact that you are devaluing your country's currency thus negatively affecting every other party in the economy?

Is this the most rewarding ability you could possibly have? Or do you prefer to do things that benefit yourself? Would you quickly become overwhelmed with demand for your healing touch?

WWYR?

Be able to tell what people really think about you?

OR

Be able to see through peoples' clothes?

Things to Consider

This could be extremely useful in many situations. But can you deal with the truth?

You might be in for some weird and wonderful sights! Are you sure this is what you want?

WWYR?

As a birthday present, be given an all expenses paid parachute jump?

OR

As a birthday present, be given an all expenses paid bungy jump?

Things to Consider

Do you like the idea of free-falling through the sky? Would you enjoy the still calmness and having nothing but air around you? Or are you too scared to even contemplate jumping out of a plane?

With this option you still get the thrill of feeling the air rush past your body as you fall. But now you have the safety of a cord to stop your descent. What if the elasticity is adjusted incorrectly? You don't have a parachute to save you.

WWYR?

Be granted four wishes of your choosing today?

OR

Be granted one wish every ten years for the rest of your life?

Things to Consider

Do you want to put in place today four things which will change the course of the rest of your life? What if you make rash decisions and set yourself off on a self-destructive path? Do you need more time to think about your wishes?

If you have decades left to live, does this choice provide better value? Or is the pace of change too slow? Will you be counting down the days, months and years to your next wish?

WWYR?

Be the only person to survive a global wipe-out of humans? **OR** Give up your life so that 5,000 humans survive the wipe-out?

Things to Consider

Have you ever fantasised about being the only person left alive on the planet? Will the novelty run out eventually? How long before you break down in despair and loneliness?

Would you sacrifice yourself so that the world could be repopulated after the wipe-out? Giving up your own life is a big choice but you are certain to be remembered as the saviour of mankind and be thought of as a sort of deity.

WWYR?

Using a razor blade, cut a six-inch gash in one of your arms?

OR

Using a razor blade, cut a six-inch gash in someone else's arm?

Things to Consider

This option is going to be unpleasant, painful and bloody for you. But at least you are doing it to yourself and no one else has to suffer. Or would you much prefer to not feel the pain?

This option involves no physical pain or injury to yourself. But what is the psychological cost of inflicting pain on someone else? Will it endure in your mind in perpetuity or do you not care?

WWYR?

Only be allowed to wear black clothes for the rest of your life?

OR

Only be allowed to wear white clothes for the rest of your life?

Things to Consider

Do you prefer to not stand out? You might be too hot in the sun and look a bit somber. Perhaps you prefer the dark, moody, slightly menacing look?

At least you will be cooler in the summer. Do you like to have a light and pure appearance? Are your white clothes going to look dirty more quickly and need to be washed more frequently?

WWYR?

Have the ability to make particular politicians tell the truth at specific points of your choosing?

OR

Have the ability to make all politicians tell the truth for the rest of time?

Things to Consider

Pick the one who you don't agree with and change what they're saying. But what if your point of view proves to be incorrect? Have you messed things up for everyone now?

At first glance this seems tempting. But is this really desirable? Or are lies necessary in certain circumstances such as during a war?

WWYR?

Be given the
solution to global   **OR**   Be given the
climate change?   solution to curing
                            cancer?

Things to Consider

Would you sell the
information? Or,
publish it
yourself? Would
anyone believe
you? Would it be
surpressed?

This would help
many people for
sure. But would it
make enough of a
difference to
warrant this
choice?

WWYR?

Spend a year of your life strapped to a bed (arms and legs immobilised)?

OR

Spend a year of your life never being able to sit or lay down?

Things to Consider

You are going to have to rely on others to feed you. What is going to happen to your muscles and fitness? On the plus side, at least you can lay back and relax. You experience no physical stress but how quickly will you tire of the situation?

Can you sleep standing up? You're going to have to if you select this option. What will the effect of gravity be on your body over a year? Will it drag you down both physically and mentally? On the plus side, you can still move around and do things.

WWYR?

Have your weight frozen in time as it is today so that you never gain or lose any?

OR

Have a random weight assigned to you once a month?

Things to Consider

Are you content with how you look and feel today? Or, at least happy enough not to gamble with it? If you choose this option, will you always be wondering what you could have looked like? Would you feel that you missed out on trying new sizes?

Would you like to experience lots of different body types? This might cost a lot of money in clothes. Every now and again you will happen upon a month in which you feel that you are perfect. Is the gamble worth it so that you have these experiences?

WWYR?

Go back in time to when you were five years old.

OR   Stick as you are?

Things to Consider

Do you wish you had done things differently? Do you wish you had made different choices and lived a different life? This is your opportunity to go back and change that.

Is meddling with the past a can of worms? Maybe you embrace all of your mistakes and consider them to be part of what makes you YOU. Or, do you relish the idea of doing it all again differently?

WWYR?

Be able to mimic all sounds with your voice?

OR

Be able to, like a chameleon, blend into any environment by clicking your fingers?

Things to Consider

How much fun could you have by making phone alert noises or the sound of approaching footsteps?

Would you hide yourself in a meeting room and hear what is being said? Or would you offer your services to the military?

WWYR?

Be able to make people's noses grow when they are telling lies?

OR

Be able to make coloured smoke come from people's noses when they are feeling contempt for you?

Things to Consider

Do you always want to hear the truth? Or do you prefer being told what you want to hear?

Do you really want to know when people feel contempt for you? Or would you prefer that this was hidden from you?

WWYR?

Be able to levitate objects?

OR

Be able to use your hands as powerful electromagnets (you can turn them on and off)?

Things to Consider

Would you use this ability to entertain people? Or to destroy things?

Would you stop cars and trains? Or steal jewellery from a distance?

WWYR?

Take part in a sword fight to the death?

OR

Take part in a pistol duel to the death?

Things to Consider

Do you like the idea of hearing metal against metal? Does the tactical aspect of sword fighting appeal to you? What if you're not victorious? Is all the drama worth it? Would a bullet get it over with more quickly? Maybe you like the drama.

Win or lose, this is going to be over in an instant. Do you prefer that idea? It's certainly more efficient than having to battle it out with a sword. Or do you think this option puts you in greater peril? At least with the sword you have a better chance of survival. Or do you?

WWYR?

Be guaranteed to live to exactly 100 years of age?

OR

Be guaranteed to live to exactly 200 years of age?

Things to Consider

Would you have had enough of life by 100? Would it be cool to make a century? You'd be part of a small club.

Would you get bored of living after you make the 100-year milestone? Bear in mind that the world will change beyond all recognition in your second century. What will your quality of life be like?

WWYR?

Be given the ability to end world hunger for a year?

OR

Be able to change the global economy to a single currency and wipe out every country's debt?

Things to Consider

You can stop any humans dying from hunger right now, for a year. Does this appeal to your sense of compassion? Or is it cruel to give false hope for a limited time?

If you rebalanced The World's economy would this prevent any and all future food shortages? Are you a long-term thinker? Or have previous experiments in this area failed because the idea is impractical?

WWYR?

Be given a diary of your life with a 500-word entry for each day that you HAVE lived?

OR

Be given a diary of your life with a 500-word entry for each day that you WILL live in the future?

Things to Consider

Would you like to look back and review your successes and failures? Are there certain memories that you don't want to revisit?

Can you resist the temptation to see your future? Would knowing it spoil future surprises?

WWYR?

Be given a movie made up of pictures of you from every day that you HAVE lived?

OR

Be given a movie made up of pictures of you from every day that you WILL live in the future?

Things to Consider

Can you bear seeing those unhappy memories that you have blocked out? Would it be worth it to relive forgotten moments that made you smile?

What if by looking into the future you see something that you don't like? Do you want to see a picture of the final day of your life?

WWYR?

Legalise ethaniasia in every country in the world?

OR

Legalise marajuana in every country in the world?

Things to Consider

Do you believe humans should be allowed to choose the time of their own death? Or do you believe that life is a gift and should never be prematurely ended?

Are you sufficiently convinced by the research that sets out the health benefits of legalisation? Or are you concerned about negative side effects?

WWYR?

For one day, live as the leader of a country?

OR

For one day, live as an internationally famous singer/musician?

Things to Consider

Is it exciting to think of what you would do with the executive powers of, say, the President of the USA? Do you really want to see behind the scenes of the corridors of power? What if it doesn't meet your expectations?

Would you like to know how it feels to be worshipped for a musical gift? Are you worried that you will enjoy the experience so much that the come-down from it will be psychologically damaging? Or would the day just be a happy memory?

WWYR?

Be able to activate sticky feet that allow you to walk along walls and ceilings like a spider? **OR** Be able to see in the dark with 100% clarity?

Things to Consider

Walking up the side of a building would be a hell of a party trick and a money-spinner. Maybe you would be tempted to become a jewel thief.

Permanent night vision might be an invaluable asset to the military, miners or search and rescue teams. Do you want to always be out at night? Will it mess up your sleeping pattern?

WWYR?

Have dinner with Hannibal Lecter?   **OR**   Have dinner with Adolf Hitler?

Things to Consider

Would you admire Lecter's intelligence or be repulsed by his anecdotes? Or both?

Hitler would certainly have some stories to tell you. But would you want to hear them?

WWYR?

Be able to walk on water?   **OR**   Be able to turn water into wine?

Things to Consider

With your water-walking ability, would you become a coast guard rescuer or a touring entertainer? How soon would you tire of having wet feet and wish you had more wine?

If you kept it quiet, you could have a free lifetime supply of wine. But if your secret got out would you become a target for intimidation by the alcohol industry?

WWYR?

Be able to
breathe out fire? **OR** Be able to
breathe out
smoke?

Things to Consider

Do you want to be known as 'The Human Dragon'? You are likely to become a well-known celebrity very quickly but what will the impact on your lungs be?

What would you use your smokey ability for? Would you create smokescreens and get up to mischief? Is this skill likely to screw up your lungs more quickly than fire breathing?

WWYR?

Have the ability to create a sonic boom at will?

OR

Have the ability to emit a strong electromagnetic pulse (EMP) at will?

Things to Consider

How would you use the startling effect of the boom? Creating thunder at will would strike fear into many. Would this distraction be most useful for good or evil pursuits?

The sending out of a strong EMP has the effect of disabled all electronic equipment within a certain radius. How would this be useful? Stopping terrorists in their tracks? Or for disabling security systems so that you can commit a crime?

WWYR?

Never need to sleep again?

OR

Have to sleep for 20 hours each day?

Things to Consider

If you never switch off, how much more productive would you be? Probably lots. But if your mind never gets the chance to reset itself through rest and dreams, will you suffer negative psychological repercussions?

If you love sleep, or have trouble sleeping, a guaranteed long slumber might seem desirable. But, would you take the guarantee even if it had to be for such a long duration?

WWYR?

From tomorrow be unmarried and single for the rest of your life?

OR

Tomorrow, be assigned a life partner via a 'lucky dip' process?

Things to Consider

Would you rather be lonely than risk a life of potential misery? Will you always be wondering what might have happened had you chosen the other option?

Would you miss company so much that you would take the risk of the random selection? What if you and your lucky dip partner are completely incompatible? Could you laugh about it and just get on with it?

WWYR?

Never be able to
close your eyes? **OR** Only be able to
open your eyes
for half an hour
per day?

Things to Consider

Can you learn to
sleep with open
eyes? Can you
really cope with
seeing
EVERYTHING all
of the time? How
much are you
going to miss the
peaceful
darkness of
closed eyes?

Could you learn
to live blind for
most of the day?
How would you
maximise that half
hour when you
have your eyes
open? Would this
choice make you
value and
appreciate your
sight more?

WWYR?

Never forget
anything ever
again?

OR

Have your
memory reset
every year on
your birthday?

Things to Consider

Being a memory
genius could be
useful. You would
be a highly
trusted employee
of any business.
But is it
sometimes useful
to forget things?
Is it healthy for
your mind to
naturally filter
and discard
things?

How would your
relationships with
others be
affected? Could
you develop a
strategy to
re-learn what you
need to know
quickly each
year? Is it going
to be a pain to
have to re-learn
all of life's basic
skills every year?

WWYR?

Be able to control two sentences that another person says per day?

OR

Be able to control everything that another person says all day, for one day, each year?

Things to Consider

How powerful would you feel knowing that you can influence two sentences per day in your favour? Are these small nudges enough though? Wll you be frustrated that you can't do more?

Would it be useful to be able to plan for a whole year and then use one person to make a series of big decisions all in one day? If it goes wrong then you are going to have to wait a whole year to have another opportunity.

WWYR?

Have the ability to drain other people's energy with your mind?

OR

Have the ability to inject energy into other people with your mind?

Things to Consider

Maybe some people are too excitable for your liking. Or, maybe you simply have times when you want someone to just go to bed and leave you alone. When a friend or loved one is hyper with nervousness or anxiety you can take some of it away.

Does it break your heart to see another person feeling down and upset? Would you like to be able to snap someone out of the lull or dip that they are in?

WWYR?

Have the ability to walk through walls?

OR

Have the ability to melt metal with your hands?

Things to Consider

Would you be tempted to become a master thief? Or, make money as an escape artist? Or would you use your powers for good and, for example, save people who are trapped in burning buildings?

Would you become a safecracker? Free prisoners for a fee? Or use your ability in a military capacity to help disable enemy equipment?

WWYR?

Be given irresistible powers of persuasion?

OR

Be given the ability to instantaneously compute probability?

Things to Consider

Do you fancy being employed as an international trade deal consultant? Or, as a hostage negotiator? Or would you use your powers to acquire things that you are not entitled to?

This ability might make you an instant hit within gambling circles. Or maybe you would keep your skill to yourself and secretly amass a fortune. Perhaps you would help government agencies to assess risks and save lives.

WWYR?

Win a lottery jackpot but have to give it all up if anyone ever asks you if you have won it?

OR

Win a lottery jackpot but, for the rest of your life, have to wear, at all times, a baseball cap that says 'I won big on the lottery'.

Things to Consider

Can you keep a secret? REALLY keep a secret? Can you live a sufficiently-modest lifestyle to not draw attention to yourself? Is the stress of the secret going to spoil your enjoyment of the money?

Is this an embarrassing proposition? Is it really THAT bad? After all, you get to enjoy the money in an open and transparent way. Will people be jealous of you and will they think the cap is austentatious?

WWYR?

Be made 5% better in all of your abilities.

OR

Be made exceptionally good at a randomly assigned skill?

Things to Consider

You would become suddenly sharper at everything you do. How would this make you feel and appear to those around you? If you choose this option will you always be wondering what it would have felt like to be exceptional at something?

We would all love to be considered to be 'exceptional' at something. But what if that something is not considered by society to be of value or use? Is this option worth it if the randomly assigned skill turns out to be a frivolous one?

WWYR?

Have GPS and SAT NAV permanently built into your head?

OR

Have invisible sunglasses fitted to your eyes which you can activate at times of your choosing by touching the side of your head?

Things to Consider

Do you want to be reassured that you will never again be lost? Or can you already get by with external devices that you own? Do you trust them? What if they fail?

This would certainly be a useful, convenient and cost-saving augmentation to your body. But some people just like wearing their shades. Are you one of them?

WWYR?

Have to wear randomly assigned clothes everyday?

OR

Have to wear the same outfit, which you can choose today, every day for the next five years?

Things to Consider

This might be comical for a while but how soon would the novelty wear off? Would people think you are super cool for being able to switch styles rapidly? Or would they think you are a show-off?

At least you know what you're choosing. Are you ok with this or will you become bored quickly? How quickly?

WWYR?

Have to listen to people speaking all of the time that you are awake?

OR

Only be able to hear any form of speech for five minutes each day?

Things to Consider

Can you cope with never having silence again and hearing constant chatter? Perhaps you would welcome the continuous conversation and enjoy the company.

Would you miss spontaneous conversation? Maybe this limited window of time would help you to focus your vocal interactions into highly-productive exchanges.

WWYR?

Be able to impersonate any living or dead person's voice perfectly?

OR

Look exactly like one person of your choosing for one day each year?

Things to Consider

Fancy having some fun on the phone? You could make a lot of people smile and laugh with this ability. Or maybe you would use your ability to talk yourself into situations that you wouldn't otherwise have access to.

Walk around like a celebrity and enjoy the feeling of fame and attention? Or transform into your partner and experience what other people say to them while you are not around? Is it morally acceptable to impersonate someone else?

WWYR?

For the rest of your life, speak with an extremely low voice?

OR

For the rest of your life, speak with an extremely high voice?

Things to Consider

Does low sound authoritative? Or does it make you sound old and boring?

Maybe only dogs can hear you. Are you likely to be made fun of?

WWYR?

For the rest of your life, speak with an extremely loud voice?

OR

For the rest of your life, speak with an extremely quiet voice?

Things to Consider

Are you happy to scare everyone and have them turn around and look at you upon every utterance? Is this going to be a curse that prevents you wanting to speak in public?

Would you struggle to be heard? Or would this cause people to stop and listen closely and intently to you?

WWYR?

Never again feel sceptical about anything?

OR

Never again feel optimistic about anything?

Things to Consider

Are you at a disadvantage if you have to take everything at face value? Or does scepticism get in the way and prevent you from taking chances that might lead to enjoyable experiences?

Choosing this option doesn't necessarily entail feeling pessimistic about things, you can feel indifference too. Does a sense of hope and future happiness get you through life? If so, will you miss it too much to give it up?

WWYR?

Have the strongest emotion that you are feeling written across your forehead at all times?

OR

Never be able to show any emotions with your face again?

Things to Consider

Are you open about your emotions? If so, will this option be easy for you to live with? Will this help others to understand you better? Is your strongest emotion likely to be anxiety due to your forehead situation?

Are there other ways you can convey emotion? Can you show people how you feel with your body language and voice? Or do you consider facial expression to be vital to fulfilling human interaction?

WWYR?

Have to live the rest of your life with a foul smell in your nose?

OR

Have to live the rest of your life with a loud noise in your ears?

Things to Consider

You might acclimatise to the odour quite quickly and stop noticing it. But it might also affect your sense of taste and cause loss of appetite.

Would this give you constant headaches or would you get used to it after a while? Would this become a form of torture and damage your perception of sound dynamics?

WWYR?

Have a one-hour conversation with Leonardo Da Vinci?

OR

Have a one-hour conversation with Plato?

Things to Consider

This guy is widely regarded as the greatest genius there has ever been, so you will have lots of questions. But would you have anything in common? What if you can tell you're boring him? Will the time then become an embarrassing drag?

The ancient philosopher was wise, for sure, and you are bound to be impressed with his rhetoric and puzzles. But would this be an enjoyable conversation? Or would it be a frustrating debate/ argument?

WWYR?

Have a selfie taken with Julius Caesar?   **OR**   Have a selfie taken with Mohammad Ali?

Things to Consider

Do you admire the man? Or do you think that his actions were selfish and ultimately led to the decline of the Roman Empire?

He considered himself to be the greatest. But was he really? Was he an annoying egomaniac or one of the greatest sportsmen to have ever lived?

WWYR?

Be given the true facts behind the JFK assassination?

OR

Know for certain whether or not extraterrestrial beings exist?

Things to Consider

This story really is one heck of a riddle. What would you do with the information? Sell it? Would anyone believe you?

If it's 'yes, they do exist' what does this mean for humanity: hope or doom? Is 'no, they don't exist' a bleak prospect? Could you cope with being the only member of the general population who knows for sure?

WWYR?

Be given a photographic memory?

OR

Instantly attain complete mastery of a foreign language of your choice?

Things to Consider

Would you find it useful to be able to visualise and recall every detail of things that you have seen? Would you become a card counter or pass lots of exams after just skimming through books?

Maybe you want to relocate to a different country and would find this useful. Or, maybe this is simply a linguistic ambition that you have always wanted to fulfill.

WWYR?

Have your past internet browsing history published to all of your friends and family?

OR

Never browse the internet again?

Things to Consider

Is there anything in there that you are worried about? How much would people really care? Isn't everyone in the same boat? Or would this be unthinkably embarrassing?

Have you ever tried living offline? Is it possible or practical these days? Maybe it would be perfectly fine. Is it worth the risk?

WWYR?

For the rest of your life only be allowed to eat a selection of fifteen dishes of your choice?

OR

For the rest of your life have all of your meals randomly assigned to you?

Things to Consider

How large is your cooking repertoire? How many dishes do you really need to not become bored yet still get the nutrition you need?

This might be exciting and novel at first. But how quickly are you going to wish you could just cook whatever you wanted? Can you cope with steak for breakfast or a slice of toast for dinner?

WWYR?

Live exactly as you are now for the rest of your life?

OR

Be placed at a random year (past or future) and situation in which to live the rest of your life?

Things to Consider

This seems like a safe option. You just carry on as you are. But would you always wonder about what could have been if you gambled?

You could end up having the time of your life, living like a king or queen. But the opposite is also true. Is it worth the risk?

WWYR?

Always laugh uncontrollably at sad moments?

OR

Always cry inconsolably when you hear something funny?

Things to Consider

This is definitely going to be embarrassing and you are very likely to offend people. What's going to happen at funerals? Will your family disown you?

There's a lot of humour around. That's going to mean many tears unless you hide away from funny things. Is that really something you want to do? Will people stop telling you jokes so as to not upset you?

WWYR?

Go three rounds
in a ring with a   **OR**   Walk across a
professional   minefield?
boxer who you
have offended?

Things to Consider

How terrified are
you going to be?
Do you bruise
easily? At least
you can see your
opponent and can
do your best to
try and avoid
them.

Every step will be
full of trepidation
because you don't
know where the
danger is. But if
you survive you
will have a great
anecdote to
share!

WWYR?

Look inside a
black hole?

OR

Be given the date
that the earth will
cease to exist?

Things to Consider

This would be a
unique experience
that no one else is
ever likely to
have again. Maybe
you will see the
secrets behind
the universe.
What if you don't
like what you
see? Should you
tell the rest of
the world what
you saw?

We all know that
the earth has a
limited lifespan.
Would you like to
be the only
person who
knows the
precise date of
its demise? Or
would this be too
sobering for
you?

WWYR?

Spend a year of your life in solitary confinement?

OR

Spend a year of your life in which every second of it is streamed live on the internet?

Things to Consider

Are you ok with your own company? Some people go a bit mad in solitary confinement. Others develop a deep understanding of themselves and experience peace.

How much do you value your privacy? Are you an attention seeker? Do you trust yourself not to do something silly whilst under constant surveillance?

WWYR?

Change history so that the Second World War never happened?

OR

Keep history exactly as it is?

Things to Consider

Would you like to be able to prevent the huge loss of life that occurred?

Do you believe that the War was necessary, maybe even inevitable, and that its legacy shapes the modern world in a beneficial way?

WWYR?

Bring back into fashion flared trousers and platform shoes?

OR

Bring back into fashion bowler hats for men and bonnets for women?

Things to Consider

Do you think the 1960s and 1970s were the best decades for fashion? Do you wish you could bring them back right now? Or do you think this sort of nostalgia is artificial and a waste of time?

These garments haven't been commonplace for a long time. Was there something nice about the formality of them? Or, does the formality put you off?

WWYR?

Commit one crime of your choice with immunity from prosecution once per year?

OR

Commit five crimes of your choice each year with a 99% chance of not being caught?

Things to Consider

If you have a year to think and plan are you more likely to use your annual opportunity in a way that maximises its effect?

You have five times the opportunity but can you cope with that small possibility that you might get caught?

WWYR?

For the rest of your life, have every choice that you are presented with decided by your mother?

OR

For the rest of your life, have every choice that you are presented with decided by a randomly-selected former teacher of yours from school?

Things to Consider

Are you comfortable with consulting your mother on everything from what clothes you are wearing today to what you are having for dinner tomorrow?

Do your old teachers know what is best for you? How well do they know you? Might they act maliciously if they don't like you?

WWYR?

For the rest of your life, live off state-issued food?

OR

For the rest of your life, be dressed in state-issued clothes?

Things to Consider

How quickly would you get bored of not having a choice? Or would you simply acclimatise and get used to it like prisoners in jail or hospital patients do?

Do you consider your clothing to be a form of self-expression? Or do you not mind and think that clothes are simply functional items?

WWYR?

Be guaranteed to have 20/20 vision for the rest of your life? **OR** Be guaranteed to never lose any teeth before you die?

Things to Consider

You'll save money on glasses and never have to worry about going blind or suffering from short- or long-sightedness.

Everyone worries about losing their teeth and having to wear dentures. How much would you like to be relieved of this worry?

WWYR?

Have a gland under your arm which grows one pearl per week?

OR

Grow saffron from your head instead of hair?

Things to Consider

You would have a steady income for the small inconvenience of having a constant growth under your arm. Does it help that the pearl is discrete and not readily visible?

This is a highly expensive spice that will guarantee you a strong income. You just have to put up with looking and smelling a bit funny. Would you wear a hat to cover it up?

WWYR?

Be able to see
through metal?   **OR**   Be able to see
                                 through skin in
                                 order to identify
                                 ailments and
                                 broken bones?

Things to Consider

Would you use
this ability to help
defuse bombs or
crack safes? Or,
use your ability to
snoop and spy?

Various scanners
are used to
detect ailments
but people need
to go to hospitals
to avail of them.
You could spot
things well in
advance of health
issues becoming
serious.

WWYR?

Live the rest of your life as a lone lighthouse operator, never allowed to step outside of the building?

OR

Live the rest of your life on a submarine that never surfaces, along with a crew of 134?

Things to Consider

Are you comfortable with your own company? Would you miss contact with others?

Do you like privacy and having quiet moments? How much would you miss being alone? Or would you be happy being constantly sociable?

WWYR?

Have a finger which can open any lock?

OR

Have a sum twice your annual income deposited into your bank account right now?

Things to Consider

Enter any building that you like. Never get locked out of your car again. Go on tour as a stage magician. Is your ability going to encourage you to commit illegal acts?

Have you got ideas about how you would invest this money? Or would have the time of your life by hosting huge parties and shopping?

WWYR?

Never have to
pay tax again?

OR

Extend your life
expectancy by
five years?

Things to Consider

How long have
you got to live?
Can you estimate
how much money
you are going to
save in your
remaining years?

Do you want to
have more time
to spend with
family and
friends? Or will
you have had
enough as you
start to
approach the
end?

WWYR?

Live the rest of
your life in a
communist
regime?

OR

Live the rest of
your life under a
totalitarian
regime?

Things to Consider

Does the theory
of a socialist,
equitable ideal
appeal to you? Is
it practical? How
have previous
experiments in
this area played
out in practice?

Things certainly
get done in this
environment. But
does power
corrupt?

WWYR?

Be able to erase any part of your memory at any time of your choosing?

OR

Be able to erase one memory once per year?

Things to Consider

You might find the desire to instantly erase bad experiences very tempting. This would relieve your stress but are bad experiences useful? Do we learn from them?

On New Year's Eve you can think back on the previous year and wipe away the memory of something you wish had never happened. By narrowing your options are you more likely to choose more carefully?

WWYR?

Never experience day-time again?   **OR**   Never experience night-time again?

Things to Consider

Would you need to take vitamin supplements to compensate for the lack of sunlight? Will you miss the heat of the sun on your skin and seeing the sunset?

Are you a night owl? Is this when you come alive? What would it be like to never experience nightlife again?

WWYR?

Have every second that you sleep streamed live on the internet?

OR

Have every toilet visit that you make streamed live on the internet (footage from the neck up only)?

Things to Consider

Do you talk in your sleep or thrash around like a mad person? Does your body make noises that you are unaware of when you sleep?

Can you keep a straight face? The viewers will be waiting for any slight change of expression. Perhaps you are an exhibitionist and love the thought of others watching you.

WWYR?

Never again be
able to doubt
yourself?

OR

Never again be
able to doubt
other people?

Things to Consider

Would others
consider you to
be annoyingly
confident? What
if you're wrong
about things? How
will you check?

Who do you
trust? Can you
afford to take
everyone at face
value? It might
feel good to
always have faith
in everyone but is
this practical?

WWYR?

Lose the ability to walk up or down stairs?

OR

Lose the ability to make left-hand turns when you are walking or driving?

Things to Consider

This is certainly doable but what adjustments would you have to make to your life? Would you have to research the stair situation of everywhere before you go there?

This is going to be quite inconvenient and will mean a lot of logistical planning before you leave the house to go anywhere. One advantage might be that you visit some places that you wouldn't have otherwise.

WWYR?

Have skin made of leather?

OR

Have live snakes attached to your head instead of hair?

Things to Consider

You might look a bit weird but, on the plus side, you are less likely to suffer cuts and bruises.

You will definitely turn heads with this look. Would you have to feed the snakes? Would they bite you or those around you? Or both? How could you deal with this?

WWYR?

Never use the internet again?

OR

Live alone forever and never step outside of your house again?

Things to Consider

Would it really be that bad? Would you read books instead? Maybe you'd be better off without being constantly notified of things.

Could you live with just the internet for company? Your food and supplies could be ordered online and you could work from home. Is this a satisfying lifestyle?

WWYR?

Shout out 'bottoms up' any time someone within five metres of you says the word 'yes'?

OR

Shout out 'mum's the word' any time someone within five metres of you says the word 'no'?

Things to Consider

How would people react to you? With confusion or with laughter?

Are you going to be thought of as quirky or annoying?

WWYR?

Have hands twice the size that they are now?   **OR**   Have feet that are twice the size that they are now?

Things to Consider

Would the benefits of being able to carry more items, with your oversized hands, outway the disbenefit of having an unusual appearance?

You will have increased stability and potentially be able to run faster. But where will you buy your shoes and how much will they cost?

WWYR?

Make every future decision by tossing a coin?

OR

Have every future decision decided for you via the majority decisions of polls of your friends and family?

Things to Consider

You have, on average, a fifty-fifty chance of every decision going in either direction. Could you come up with a clever technique of breaking down decisions into smaller elements to mitigate the random effect?

Do you really want to forgo your privacy and have your loved ones know the things that you are deciding? On the plus side, these people should have your best interests at heart.

WWYR?

Have the same
100 music tracks
on a loop in your
head for the rest
of your life?

OR

Never hear
another musical
track again?

Things to Consider

At first glance
this seems
attractive as at
least you will have
some music to
listen to. But, in
time, would the
constant loop
become more like
torture than
pleasure?

Can you cope
without music?
How quickly would
you adjust? Is
having no music in
your life
preferable to a
constant loop?

WWYR?

Address the nation, via live internet stream, for one hour on a subject that is handed to you as you walk on stage?

OR

Agree to shorten your life by two years?

Things to Consider

How much do you enjoy public speaking? Are you good at 'winging it' when you are under pressure? Does public speaking make you feel uncomfortable and do you avoid it at all costs?

The years at the end of your life are the worst ones, aren't they? Would you give up two of these years to not have to go through the pain of public speaking?

WWYR?

Betray your country by passing state secrets to a foreign nation once a month for a year?

OR

Make your home a safehouse for international terrorists for two nights?

Things to Consider

Could you live with yourself if you commit multiple acts of treason? How confident are you that you won't be caught? You will, of course, be handsomely remunerated for your deceit.

The awkward situation will be over quickly but would you feel morally compromised for doing what you've done?

WWYR?

Spend 48 hours in a sewer? **OR** Sleep in a tent for six months?

Things to Consider

Can you cope with rats? Do foul odours make you feel sick? Could you sleep down there? Or even sit down in a sewer? Would 48 hours seem like an eternity?

You will be reasonably comfortable, compared to the alternative, but is six months too long a period to be away from a bed?

WWYR?

Mispronounce every tenth word that you say?

OR

Have every other word that you say silenced so that your speech appears oddly broken to the listener?

Things to Consider

Can you plan ahead so that the effect of the tenth word is not so great? Or would you just learn to live with the affliction and explain the situation to everyone you encounter?

Would you carry around a pen and paper or tablet computer to write messages on? Or would you try to talk normally and hope that people accept your new situation?

WWYR?

Have surgery on your brain so that you feel no pain for the rest of your life?

OR

Have surgery on your brain so that you increase your intelligence?

Things to Consider

Everyone tries to avoid pain, nobody enjoys it. But is it also useful?

Would you risk having a procedure to feel a bit sharper? It could be very quick and easy. But are super-smart people more or less happy than averagely-smart people?

WWYR?

Never kiss anyone ever again?

OR

Have a life-changing lottery win?

Things to Consider

Is living without this form of affection unimaginable to you? Or are you not too bothered? Maybe you have already done all of the kissing that you want to.

What would you do with the money? Would you give up kissing for a large amount of cash?

WWYR?

Lay in a bath of spiders for 20 minutes?

OR

Lay in a bath of beetles for 60 minutes?

Things to Consider

They say the reason people don't like spiders is the fact that their movements are unpredictable. Would you pick the 20 minute option to get it over with more quickly?

At least beetles move in predictable patterns. But is one hour too long to endure? Or maybe you like having insects crawl around your body.

WWYR?

Never eat bread again?   **OR**   Never eat cheese again?

Things to Consider

No more sandwiches. No more pizza. No more toast. No more bagels or bruschetta. Can you cope with that?

No more mac and cheese. No more cheese on toast. No more cauliflower cheese or baked brie. Does this sound horrific or are you not bothered?

WWYR?

Introduce compulsory national service of five years for all 18 year olds?

OR

Remove all capability and knowledge of nuclear warfare from the world?

Things to Consider

Do you think this would instill a valuable sense of discipline in young people? Or might it spoil the end of adolescence?

Does nuclear warfare make the future of the world more precarious? Or does the mutually assured destruction thing, in a way, make us safer?

WWYR?

Spend two years
mastering circus
skills?

OR

Spend five years
mastering card
tricks?

Things to Consider

You would end up
with a set of
skills including: lion
taming, juggling,
trapeze, tightrope
walking, knife
throwing and fire
breathing.

Make a fortune
as a stage
performer? Or
maybe you would
be tempted to
hustle
unsuspecting
passersby on the
street? Will the
longer investment
in time yield a
greater reward?

WWYR?

Spend one month as a sniper camped out behind enemy lines?

OR

Spend one month as a general commanding troops who are engaged in battle?

Things to Consider

Does the tension and excitement of playing a vital part in frontline combat appeal to you?

Do you want to be the supremo in the background who moves troops around like chess pieces?

WWYR?

Live in a treehouse for the rest of your life?

OR

Live in an underground bunker for the rest of your life?

Things to Consider

Are you good on a ladder? Can you cope with all of the maintenance that will be required to ensure that your house doesn't fall to the ground?

How much would you miss the daylight? Maybe you would feel safe since hurricanes, tornadoes and generally poor weather won't affect you.

WWYR?

Eat a whole lemon live on an internet video stream?

OR

Eat a whole onion live on an internet video stream?

Things to Consider

Can you really get through all of this bitterness, including the skin, without being sick? Would the large volume of acid damage your stomach?

Onions are not just sour and bitter, they contain a lot of heat and are certain to make your eyes water. Onion skin is very dry and is difficult to eat.

WWYR?

For the rest of your life, have peoples' faces blanked out from your view?

OR

For the rest of your life, have all foods taste the same to you?

Things to Consider

This will be inconvenient but at least you can still talk to everyone. Are you bad at remembering faces anyway? How much will you miss seeing facial expressions?

Do you savour your food or think of it as just fuel? Will you miss different flavours or is eating an inconvenience to you and something that slows you down?

WWYR?

Be put to death by lethal injection? **OR** Be put to death by facing a firing squad?

Things to Consider

One small pin prick and it's all over. This is a relatively private affair: just you and a doctor.

There is much more drama involved in this method. But there are many more witnesses to your death.

WWYR?

Be abducted by aliens with a 50% chance that they will return you to earth?

OR

Nominate a close family member to be abducted by aliens with a 50% chance that they will be returned to earth?

Things to Consider

Are you willing to take the chance yourself? Or do you consider yourself to be the person who needs to remain and hold the family together?

Who do you pick? The family member who contributes the least? What will the rest of your family think of you if you nominate someone else?

WWYR?

Have to eat two insects each day? **OR** Have to eat one live goldfish per week?

Things to Consider

Insects are crunchy but at least they are small. Which insects would you choose? Flies? Spiders? Ants? Earwigs?

Goldfish are bigger but they have a slimy texture and will wriggle around in your mouth. Would you chew or swallow it whole? If the latter, would it still be alive in your stomach?

WWYR?

Spend one week each year handcuffed to a random stranger?

OR

Spend one week each year handcuffed to your least favourite teacher from school?

Things to Consider

You might get on like a house on fire, or it might be a complete nightmare. Maybe you will meet your new best friend, or maybe it will end in a fight.

At least you know each other. It's going to be horrible but is it better than taking a chance with a random stranger?

WWYR?

For one night each week, sleep on a bed of nails? **OR** For one night each week, sleep in an ice bath?

Things to Consider

Can you keep still and spread your weight evenly? You will need to get used to not moving during the night so that you don't injure yourself.

Can your body get used to this? Will it irreparably damage your health or might it turn out to be good for you?

WWYR?

Be able to heal the sick with one touch? **OR** Be able to raise the dead with one touch?

Things to Consider

You could be a real-life healer which will bring you fame and fortune. You might need lots of security around you to keep you safe from the huge demand for your touch.

How do we know that the dead want to be raised? Will their families be happy with this? How would you gain consent? Would people view you as a hero or as a witch?

WWYR?

Be able to talk to
ghosts?

OR

Be able to talk to
animals?

Things to Consider

Would you earn
money by passing
messages from
families to their
deceased
relatives? Would
anyone believe
that your gift
was real and
would this
matter?

Would this be
fun? Or would it
be extremely
boring and tedious
to hear the same
things over and
over again? Might
you learn that
animals hate
humans and find
their behaviour
contemptuous?
What then?

WWYR?

Have skin that always smells of fish? **OR** Have skin that always smells of garlic?

Things to Consider

Would you eat lots of fish-based dishes in an attempt to explain away your natural odour?

Would you really mind smelling of garlic? It's strong, sure, but some people love the fragrance. It's in so much of the food we eat that people might not even notice.

WWYR?

Never be able to offend anyone ever again? **OR** Never have to worry about money ever again?

Things to Consider

People seem to spend an enormous amount of time worrying about causing offence. How much of a benefit to you would it be to be relieved of this burden?

Does thinking about money take up a lot of your time and would you be more productive if you weren't focussed on it? Or are you already financially secure for life?

174

WWYR?

Remember every single one of your dreams in vivid detail?

OR

Never be able to remember any of your dreams ever again?

Things to Consider

Some people believe that our dreams tell us about unresolved conflicts in our minds. Do you need to learn from certain dreams in order to move on? What is the role of recurring dreams in the mind? Are they trying to tell us something?

Do you believe that dreams are an irrelevant distraction and are best forgotten? Or do you enjoy thinking back on the adventures that your mind has taken you on? Has a dream ever led to an idea that you wouldn't have thought of whilst awake?

WWYR?

For the rest of your life, have to cook all of your food from scratch?

OR

For the rest of your life, never be allowed to cook anything from scratch?

Things to Consider

Would this be painful for you and too time-consuming? Do you have much to learn and many internet videos to watch in order to get up to speed? Or will this be a pleasure for you and a chance to refine your existing skills?

Maybe this sounds like an ideal scenario for you. Perhaps you like to pop all of your food in the microwave and let it do the work for you. Or are you creative in the kitchen? Would you miss being able to invent your own recipes?

WWYR?

Be transported back to the Second World War and be a radio operator?

OR

Be transported back to the Second World War and be a tank driver?

Things to Consider

Prefer to be away from the front line? Want to be the guy in the background who provides vital communications links? It might sound like fun but you are a target for the enemy who will want to shut down your transmissions before they attack

Prefer the drama of rolling across the countryside in a fortified metal box? Think about this: you don't know which side you will be on or exactly when and where you will be transported to.

WWYR?

As a circus performer, be a tightrope walker?

OR

As a circus performer, be the person who has knives thrown at them?

Things to Consider

This is quite a skill to master and looks very impressive. Would you like being the centre of attention and performing in the knowledge that you have a safety net below you?

This is a very passive role, you simply have to stay still. So, it's an easy job but can you cope with the anxiety and stress of waiting for mistakes to happen? They must happen sometimes.

WWYR?

Never make any more new friends?

OR

Have a fresh group of friends randomly assigned to you once a year?

Things to Consider

Are you the sort of person who keeps only a handful of lifelong friends? Are you happy with what you've got and don't want to risk changing them?

Do you enjoy meeting new people often, exploring their opinions and getting to know them? What if you just don't get along? Might there be cultural or linguistic barriers in the way with the random assignment system?

WWYR?

Involuntarily shout 'oh for goodness sake' whenever you hear the word 'please'?

OR

Involuntarily shout 'dream on' whenever you hear the phrase 'thank you'?

Things to Consider

'Please' is uttered a lot in polite society. You have the potential to turn many heads and cause great confusion without even trying. Or could you devise a clever way to get around this problem?

'Thank you' is often the phrase that is used to denote the end of an interaction. Your 'dream on' remark breaks this rule and invites further conversation. Is this going to be funny or awkward?

WWYR?

Eat only Chinese food for the rest of your life? **OR** Eat only Italian food for the rest of your life?

Things to Consider

If you like rice, noodles and soy sauce then this might be the option for you. Are you good with chopsticks?

This is going to mean lots of bread, olive oil, pasta and tomatoes. Does this sound good to you?

WWYR?

For six months of the year live in a tent in the Sahara desert?

OR

For six months of the year live on a fishing trawler?

Things to Consider

Can you take the heat and the arid, dry environment? Does the idea of being in a sandstorm terrify or excite you?

You will have to pull your weight and do your bit as part of the crew. This is going to be hard, wet and windy work. But maybe you love the ocean and this is the perfect life for you.

WWYR?

Have the wisdom
of an owl?   **OR**   Have the patience
                            of a saint?

Things to Consider

Do you like the
thought of being
viewed as wise
and having people
coming to you
for advice about
their lives?

Are you easily
frustrated? Do
you find it hard
to wait for
things? Does this
cause you
anxiety? Would
you like to be
able to wait, relax
and just go with
the flow without
becoming
impatient?

WWYR?

Never be allowed to wear deodorant again?

OR

Never be allowed to shave any part of your body again?

Things to Consider

Could you come up with a clever way to mask your natural scent? Or would you simply socialise a lot less for fear of ridicule?

Is it going to be a nuisance having a hairy face, legs and armpits? Or do you like to be natural anyway? Would you get used to this situation quickly? How much time would you save each day?

WWYR?

Be able to breathe under water?

OR

Be able to easily tolerate any temperature without suffering any impact on your health?

Things to Consider

Would you market yourself as the world's most sought-after deep sea diver? Or you could use your gift for pleasure by exploring shipwrecks and studying coral?

You could fly to the sun to see what it's like or go for a swim in an active volcano. Does this sound like fun?

WWYR?

Spend a night locked in a room with a rat? **OR** Spend the night locked in a room with a goose?

Things to Consider

These guys can get nasty and bite you. They also spread disease. Could you get any sleep?

Could you put up with the sound of relentless squawking? Can you cope with it flapping around and feathers flying all around the room?

WWYR?

Be able to change the TV channel by just thinking about it?

OR

Be able to, by thinking about it, make one person per day look behind them for two seconds, once per day?

Things to Consider

This would be pretty convenient. You would never have to worry about losing the remote control or changing its batteries. You could have fun changing other people's TV channels as you walk past their houses.

If you see someone that you find attractive you could make them see you and notice you. Also, you could prevent accidents from happening or make someone walk into a dangerous situation.

WWYR?

Be able to move objects with your mind?   **OR**   Be able to move people with your words?

Things to Consider

This is known as telekinesis and presents limitless possibilities. You could stop meteorites from hitting the earth and be the ultimate hero. Or, you could amuse yourself by causing minor accidents in restaurants.

They say the pen is mightier than the sword. Would you like to be remembered as one of the world's greatest novelists or poets?

WWYR?

Never watch another sporting event again? **OR** Never watch another film again?

Things to Consider

How important is sport to you? Would losing it be too much to bear? On the other hand, how much more productive time would you have if you didn't spend so much of your week watching sport?

How many films do you watch in a year? How often do you visit the cinema? Would you miss those exciting moments when the plot thickens or twists? Would you miss being moved to tears and brought to the edge of your seat?

WWYR?

Work as an assassin for the rest of your life?   **OR**   Work as an underground sewer cleaner for the rest of your life?

Things to Consider

Can you take the stress of always looking over your shoulder and waiting to be caught? Can you cope with committing multiple immoral acts? How will this affect your mental wellbeing? At least you will be well paid and each job will be over quickly.

There will be a lot less stress involved with this choice. It will, however, be unpleasant and may be just as damaging to your mental health. Or maybe you relish the thought of carrying out this vital work. Afterall, somebody has to do it.

WWYR?

Wash by having only showers for the rest of your life?

OR

Wash by having only baths for the rest of your life?

Things to Consider

Showers are quick and efficient. You will save time and your water bills will be lower. But will you miss the luxury of lying in the bath and relaxing?

This choice will cost you more money in water bills and you might be uncomfortable with the thought of contributing to climate change. But it does feel really good to be submerged in warm water?

WWYR?

Be given 20 times your annual salary as a gift but lose a randomly selected one of your senses?

OR

Be given 50 times your annual salary as a gift but lose a randomly selected one of your limbs?

Things to Consider

This is certainly a lot of money but are you prepared to gamble with your senses? As soon as you choose this option one of the following senses ceases to function: sight, hearing, sense of smell, taste or touch.

This is a hell of a lot of money to be given but how badly do you want it? Do you want it enough to give up one of your arms or legs? What if you lose your dominant arm, the one with your writing hand at the end of it?

WWYR?

For the rest of your life, eat only Indian takeaway food?

OR

For the rest of your life, eat only Chinese takeaway food?

Things to Consider

Are you a fan of spice? If not this might not be the correct choice for you. However, if you love rich curries then you will be in heaven. Or will eating nothing but Indian food make you sick of it?

This choice is going to mean eating lots of fried rice, curries, sweet and sour dishes, noodles and spring rolls? Does this sound tempting or are you going to get bored of all of the prawn crackers?

WWYR?

Spend the rest of your career working for an international illegal drugs baron?

OR

Spend the rest of your career working for an international illegal arms dealer?

Things to Consider

These guys are notorious for their lack of patience. One wrong move and you could be made to 'vanish' very quickly. You will probably make lots of money but can you cope with the stress?

Does it sound tempting to not have to have a 'real' eight hour per day job? All you have to do is match up some buyers with some sellers. It sounds easy but how would it feel to know that you are complicit in facilitating immoral transactions?

WWYR?

Have to eat the same breakfast every day for the rest of your life?

OR

Have to eat the same lunch every day for the rest of your life?

Things to Consider

Is breakfast the most important meal of the day? Is it important to have variety to maintain your health? Do you think breakfast is boring and are happy to have a bowl of cereal or a couple of pieces of toast every day?

After you finish all of your morning tasks do you like to be rewarded with a tasty lunch? If so, would you be content to have the same sandwich, or bowl of pasta, every day?

WWYR?

Live the rest of
your life without
access to a
kitchen?

OR

Live the rest of
your life without
access to a
bathroom?

Things to Consider

Without the ability
to cook would
you have to live
on takeaway
food and eat out
regularly? Would
this be cost
effective?

Can you wash at
your place of
work or at your
local leisure
centre? How are
you going to
dispose of your
bodily waste
products?

WWYR?

Have your hair grow at twice its usual speed?

OR

Have fingernails and toenails that grow at twice their usual speed?

Things to Consider

This is going to mean twice as many trips to the hairdressers which will cost you money. Or maybe you are happy to get used to having longer hair.

Do you think cutting your nails is a pain at the moment? How would you feel about having to do it twice as often? Maybe you like having long nails and would welcome broken nails growing back more quickly.

WWYR?

Never feel
enthusiasm again?   **OR**   Always feel
either too warm
or too cold?

Things to Consider

How would you
feel if not
enthusiastic?
Apathetic?
Neutral?
Nonplussed?

Would you
acclimatise to this
form of
continuous
discomfort?
Would it have a
negative impact
on your health?

WWYR?

Have to sing every tenth word that you were going to say?

OR

Instead of saying every fiftieth word that you were planning to utter, have to shout 'cock a doodle doo!'

Things to Consider

This will be embarrassing but would your friends, family and colleagues soon get used to it? Would you avoid going out to bars and restaurants? Or would you go and just try to not speak?

This could be an unbearable affliction. Or, you might choose to own it. You might become a celebrity and passersby may refer to you as 'The 'Cock a doodle doo Guy'. Do you want fame if this is the price?

WWYR?

Never experience **OR** Never experience
nostalgia again? surprise again?

Things to Consider

Do you enjoy looking back to your childhood and remembering how things used to be? Do old television programmes bring back happy memories? By choosing this option you are saying goodbye to those feelings.

There is nothing quite like the feeling of having your reality jolted and suddenly experiencing something that you weren't expecting. Could you choose to live without this thrill?

WWYR?

Never again lose track of time?

OR

Never again be allowed to be lost in a daydream?

Things to Consider

Being rooted in the present has advantages. You are much less likely to be late for meetings, for example. However, boring things are much more likely to drag since you are constantly aware of the passing of time.

Do you ever allow your mind to wander off into previously unvisited thoughts? Is this state where your ideas come from? Does this mental wandering help you to tolerate long journeys and help you sleep? What would life be like without it?

WWYR?

For the rest of your life halve the size of all of the meal portions that you eat now?

OR

For the rest of your life double the size of all of the meal portions that you eat now?

Things to Consider

Do you already over eat? If so, will this be easy? Or do you have a high metabolism and need lots of fuel?

This sounds like fun at first but what would the consequences be? Rapid weight gain and indigestion? Would you have to adjust your exercise regime to compensate for the additional calories?

WWYR?

Never again be able to feel pride?

OR

Never again be able to feel empathy?

Things to Consider

Some people think that pride is an undesirable emotion that is connected to arrogance and an inflation of self worth. Others point to the value of pride in one's country, for example. What are you proud of? What would life be like without this sensation?

Feeling empathy with others can be a strain. When they are struggling you struggle a little bit too. So, should you delete this feeling? Be careful since some think an inability to empathise is connected to sociopathy.

WWYR?

Choose a piece of music that exemplifies humankind to send into space for aliens to find

OR

Choose a book that exemplifies humankind to send into space for aliens to find?

Things to Consider

Do you consider music to be a uniquely human art form that represents the species fairly? Can animals be said to make music? If so, is this the best choice?

Are books a fair representation of the human species? Is this level of linguistic sophistication unique to humans? In any case, could aliens decode and understand the words?

WWYR?

Share a meal with Abraham Lincoln?　**OR**　Take a road trip with John F Kennedy?

Things to Consider

What would you talk to Lincoln about over dinner? The American Civil War? Emancipation of slaves? How he became the President of the USA?

Would you like to know Kennedy's thoughts on his own assassination? Maybe you are more interested in the reforms he was suggesting such as his proposals for changes to the Federal Reserve or his thoughts on breaking up the CIA.

WWYR?

Have sausages instead of fingers?

OR

Have prawns instead of toes?

Things to Consider

Would you be tempted to eat your fingers? What would this do to your dexterity? Would having no fingerprints be an advantage or a disadvantage?

If you like seafood then you may be tempted to have a nibble on your toes. If they grow back fairly quickly then would you be tempted to have a steady supply of prawns? Or would it feel weird to eat your own toes?

WWYR?

Have to drink your own urine once per week?

OR

Have to eat your own excrement once per month?

Things to Consider

Some say this is good for you and has a purifying effect on the body. Others point out the pungent aroma and brackish flavour. Once a week seems like quite a lot but is this better than the alternative?

Once a month is less often than the other option but is the thought of this duty too horrific to contemplate? You have to perform the task 12 times per year. Is that 12 times too many for you?

WWYR?

Never see the
sea again?

OR

Never see the
sky again?

Things to Consider

Is the sea a
source of
comfort to you?
Do you enjoy its
calming rhythm?
Does it bring
back memories
from your
childhood? How
much would you
miss it? Maybe
you have never
seen the sea and
so wouldn't miss it
at all.

Do you enjoy
seeing shapes in
the clouds? Do
the stars provide
a source of
wonder and
fascination for
you? If so, can
you give this all up
just so that you
can see the sea?

WWYR?

Walk for a week in a random person's shoes?   **OR**   Run a marathon with no shoes?

Things to Consider

Choosing this option will mean that you are given a random pair of shoes of a random size. What if they are too big or too small? What if you receive shoes that are completely inappropriate for your day-to-day life? At least it's only for a week.

This is going to hurt and your feet may take some time to recover. Plenty of others have done this in the past so it is achievable. How's your fitness? Is running a marathon going to take you a long time?

WWYR?

Have to walk on all fours for two hours per day? **OR** Have to do a star jump each time you hear the word 'it'?

Things to Consider

You can still get around. It's just going to be a bit uncomfortable for two hours each day.
Perhaps it will be good exercise. Or maybe you will end up with pains in your back.

'It' is one of the most commonly used words in the English language. If you choose this option you need to prepare to perform a lot of star jumps.

WWYR?

Be able to transform your body into a car, and back again, at will?

OR

Be able to transform your body into an aeroplane, and back again, at will?

Things to Consider

As most of the journeys that you undertake are probably land-based, is this the best option for you? Or will you always be dreaming of the chance to fly that you gave up?

Do you want to fly like a bird? Does the idea of defying gravity appeal to you? Are you going to be pestered by people who want to come with you on your flights?

WWYR?

Have a number one music single once in your life?

OR

Have one social media post go viral once a year for the rest of your life?

Things to Consider

You will be part of musical history. Your song will probably be played on the radio for decades to come. But, in the modern world, are the music charts as important as they were in, say, the 1960s, 70s, 80s or 90s?

Having a viral post is a rare privilege. This can bring fame and fortune overnight. They are, however, forgotten very quickly as browers of the internet move on to their next whim.

WWYR?

Be stuck in a lift, on your own, for 24 hours?

OR

Be stuck in a lift with five other people that you don't know for 12 hours?

Things to Consider

A whole day is a long time to be trapped in a small area. You are likely to be bored, scared and dehydrated. But at least you can lay down and relax.

So that's six people in total stuck together. There won't be any room to stretch out and be comfortable. Would the company of strangers annoy you or give you comfort?

WWYR?

Be stuck in a time loop that restarts every five years from tomorrow?

OR

Be stuck in a five-year time loop that restarts in five years' time?

Things to Consider

From tomorrow you'll be reliving the past five years again and again. Do you consider this to be a repetitive nightmare? Or have the last five years been a pleasure?

How differently will you live your life in the next five years given the knowledge that these years will be repeated over and over again?

WWYR?

Back Artificial Intelligence (AI) as the future of our civilisation and redirect 100% of your Country's defence budget towards its research?

OR

Ban all AI research?

Things to Consider

Is the advance of AI inevitable? Are we going to be better off as a species if we accept the idea that the superior intelligence of AI will make better decisions than we humans do?

Do you think we are heading for a distopian disaster by allowing AI to advance to the point where we can't control it? Given the choice, would you stop it now before it's too late?

WWYR?

Have a completely open and free internet forever? **OR** Introduce an international internet censorship committee to decide who gets to see what?

Things to Consider

Are freedom of speech and expression the most important things? Are we better off because of the internet? If so, should access to it be a human right and made free to all citizens of the world?

Is it unrealistic to think that the internet is used only for the benefit of mankind? What about all of the criminal activity and exploitation that occurs online? Should regulators step in? Can they be trusted?

WWYR?

Have open, free
access to wifi
everywhere for
everyone?

OR

Make everyone
pay for their
own private
access to the
web?

Things to Consider

Does it seem silly
to you that
everyone pays
for their own
connection? If
we're all expected
to be able to do
things online then
surely it makes
sense to make it
open and free.

Is it safer to pay
for your own
connection? Does
this help to
disassociate your
own activity
from those of
everyone else?
Does this system
make it easier to
catch criminals
by tracing their
movements via
their internet
service
providers?

WWYR?

Introduce a scheme which 'deactivates' all humans at the age of 75 to help control global population growth?

OR

Legalise euthanasia across the globe?

Things to Consider

Would we be less stressed if we knew that we would stop at a certain age? Or, would this system encourage reckless living? Is there any point in looking after yourself if you're going to die at 75?

Should human beings have the right to decide when they want to die? Is this a simpler means of controlling population growth? Or is it a big can of worms with unforeseen consequences?

WWYR?

Introduce a law which states that politicians will be automatically removed from office and imprisoned if found to be not telling the truth?

OR

Introduce a law which makes voting in all elections compulsory (failure to comply carries a fine equal to 30% of your annual earnings).

Things to Consider

Would this stop all the deceit, lies and misdirection that you suspect is going on? Or, does the public need to be lied to sometimes? Do politicians lie during a crisis? Is this ok?

Will this system help to deliver a clearer, more inclusive version of democracy? What if you disagree with democracy? Will you feel violated if you are forced to vote?

WWYR?

Have to wear only clothes that you have made yourself?

OR

Have to cut your own hair, without using a mirror, for the rest of your life?

Things to Consider

Are you handy with a sewing machine? Are you an expert with a needle and thread? If so this might be a lot of fun for you. Or, are you too busy and inexperienced to mess around with this sort of task?

Could you own this and confidently go around feeling that your hairstyle is quirky? Or, are you never going to leave the house again for fear of ridicule?

WWYR?

See what would happen if no one turned out to vote in the two next elections?

OR

See what would happen if everyone withdrew all of their money from the banks?

Things to Consider

Would this mean that the Government is dissolved and there would be a return to being ruled by an overlord or monarch?

Would the economy collapse? Would this be a bad thing or is it an opportunity to reset and start again?

WWYR?

Have to say 'yes' to the next ten offers that you are presented with?

OR

Have to say 'no' to the next ten offers that you are presented with?

Things to Consider

Are you going to jump at the opportunity to be taken on an adventure that you have no control over? Or are you risk averse and prefer to not take chances?

Choosing this option will keep you rooted in the status quo. This is safe but will you spend the rest of your life wondering what would have happened if you'd said yes?

WWYR?

Have your thoughts displayed over your head at all times from now onwards?

OR

Have your deepest secrets from the past displayed over your head at all times?

Things to Consider

Are you happy for people to see what you think of them? What if your thoughts are a bit weird or unconventional? Do you want everyone to know?

Have you got something dark in your past that no one knows about? It might be embarrassing for everyone to read these things. But might it also help to unburden you of the secrets?

WWYR?

Drink a glass of vegetable oil?

OR

Drink a glass of water from the toilet?

Things to Consider

Can you tolerate the thick, viscous liquid running down your throat and into your stomach?

This is probably going to be physically easier to drink. But what is it going to do to your health?

WWYR?

Increase your average happiness, for the rest of your life, by 5% but shorten your lifespan by 5%?

OR

Increase your lifespan by 5% but reduce your average happiness, for the rest of your life, by 5%?

Things to Consider

Do you think that quality of life is more important than the length of your life? Would you rather be a bit happier each day than live a bit longer?

Is it all about survival for you? Do you want to keep going for as long as possible, even if you are a bit less happy as a result?

WWYR?

Change your head to a randomly assigned one? **OR** Change your body to a randomly assigned one?

Things to Consider

Are you not happy with your face and hair? Would you like to have an opportunity to change them? It is worth the risk or is this a case of 'better the devil you know'?

Are you fed up with your body? If you gamble, you could end up with a statuesque physique. Equally, you may also end up with something entirely inappropriate.

WWYR?

Lose the ability to taste sweetness ever again?

OR

Lose the ability to taste bitterness ever again?

Things to Consider

Can you give up the pleasure you get from confectionary, desserts and jam? You might miss these but would it stop you eating unhealthy, sugary foods? Would this benefit your health?

How much would you miss the taste of beer, citrus fruits and chocolate? If you remove this group of tastes would you be able to compensate by eating other things?

WWYR?

Never hear another human voice again?

OR

Hear human voices every second of every day for the rest of your life?

Things to Consider

Would you miss conversation and debating WWYR questions? Or are you happy with your own internal monologue?

By selecting this option you are ensuring that you will always have company around you. Would you love this or would it make you crave quietness? Can you sleep with endless chatter around you? Would you train yourself to, at will, block out the sound?

WWYR?

Take a trip in a   **OR**   Drive one lap in a
hot air balloon?   Formula One car?

Things to Consider

This is likely to be an all-day event and you will have to do your bit to help the crew. But once you are in the air you can enjoy a long, slow, peaceful cruise across the sky.

Do you like adrenaline-fuelled adventure and high-speed, G-force thrills? If so, this might be the choice for you. On the down side, the experience will be over very quickly.

WWYR?

Be able to communicate with birds?

OR

Be able to communicate with insects?

Things to Consider

We can hear birds chattering away all of the time. Have you ever wondered what they are saying? Maybe they know something that we don't. This is your chance to find out.

There are an estimated 10 quintilian (10,000,000,000,000,000,000) insects on the planet at any one time. What would you do if you could mobilise an army of this number?

WWYR?

Ban mobile phones **OR** Ban smoking in
in public spaces?   public spaces?

Things to Consider

Do you find it rude and distracting when those around you are on their phones all of the time? Do you think that the presence of phones in public is eroding social skills and interaction? Or, do we need to accept that interaction with phones is a way of life now?

Should people only be allowed to smoke in their own homes? Does it offend you to breathe in other peoples' smoke? Or, maybe you love smoking and wish that it was more prevalent in society.

WWYR?

Communicate
using only dance?   **OR**   Communicate
                                     using only rap?

Things to Consider

How good are
you at throwing
shapes? Good
enough to convey
what you mean
and want? Is this
going to be very
tiring? Will one
side effect be
that you become
super fit?

In choosing this
option you will at
least be able to
use words. Will
people think that
your rhymes are
amazing or will
they find you
tiresome and
annoying?

WWYR?

Not be able to watch television ever again?

OR

Not be able to listen to the radio ever again?

Things to Consider

Do you spend your evenings glued to the box? Does it seem unthinkable to never be able to do that again? Would you have more free time to do other things? Maybe you could take up reading or find a new hobby?

Are you more of an audio lover? Do you potter around the house listening to the tunes, banter, dramas and documentaries on the wireless? Would your life lose some of its colour without the radio? Or could you switch to listening to podcasts?

WWYR?

Never play a game, of any sort, again?

OR

Lose your sense of smell?

Things to Consider

No card games, board games and no more rolling of dice. No more football, snooker or tennis. Would you miss the challenge of trying to win? Or, do you hate competition and would be glad to see the back of it?

Never smell aftershave or perfume again. Never enjoy the fresh aroma of cut grass or the invigorating scent of the shore? Can you really give this up? Maybe you are more of a visual person and don't care about losing your sense of smell.

WWYR?

Have to bark like a dog every time you agree with something?

OR

Have to touch your toes every time you disagree with something?

Things to Consider

This is going to be difficult to explain away. Perhaps you would have to be upfront with everyone you encounter and forewarn them. Are you happy with people talking about you behind your back? Or, do you think barking is cool and are happy to be different?

This is possibly easier to get away with but is it going to be inconvenient for you? How many things do you disagree with during the day? Probably more than you think. Have you considered the impact this will have on your back over time?

WWYR?

Erase the Beatles from history?

OR

Erase the Rolling Stones from history?

Things to Consider

It seems unthinkable to even consider this but what if they didn't exist? What direction would popular music have taken? It may have taken a different, exciting turn for the better. Or not.

This band spent a much longer time together than the Beatles, released many more albums and performed more concerts. So, did the Stones have a greater impact on popular music than the Beatles?

WWYR?

Make yourself fall asleep by touching the tip of your nose three times with your one of your little fingers?

OR

Be able to rewind, delete and re-do five minutes of each day?

Things to Consider

Do you struggle to sleep? Is the ability to simply turn yourself off at night exactly what you need? The three-tap feature is designed to stop you accidently putting yourself to sleep at an unwanted time.

Maybe you burned your toast, lost your wallet or offended someone with an unintended faux-pas. Would this ability make you over confident and carefree?

WWYR?

Live fast and die young?   **OR**   Live slow and die old?

Things to Consider

Do you prefer the thought of partying hard and going out with a bang at a relatively young age?

Are you more inclined to play a long game, take your time, savour life and live to a ripe old age?

WWYR?

Only be allowed to
wear shorts on
your legs?

OR

Never be allowed
to wear shorts
again?

Things to Consider

This is perfect
for the summer
months but it's
bound to be a
nuisance when the
rain is pouring
down or there is
snow on the
ground.

Are you going to
be sweaty and
sticky in the sun?
Maybe you don't
like your legs and
are happy to
keep them
covered up.

WWYR?

Be a professional   **OR**   Be a professional
tennis player?   snooker player?

Things to Consider

Do you like the
thought of hitting
tennis balls at
over 100mph,
playing a crafty
drop shot or a
raking lob? Or is
the stop-start
nature of tennis
a bit annoying to
you?

Does this precise,
technical and
tactical cue sport
appeal to you? Or
is it too slow and
boring to keep
you interested?

240

WWYR?

Be in the next   **OR**   Be in the next
Star Wars movie?   Bond movie?

Things to Consider

These films have
a huge cult
following around
the world. Would
it matter what
sort of
character you
were? What if
you were playing
a droid and no
one could see
that it was you
under your
costume?

This is a classic
set of movies
which seem to
last the test of
time. Being
involved will
certainly
guarantee you a
place in movie
history.

WWYR?

Be obscenely wealthy but everyone has a low opinion of you?

OR

Live in extreme poverty but everyone thinks of you as one of the greatest humans to have ever lived?

Things to Consider

Have as much money as you want and do whatever your heart desires. Is this what is important to you? Are you happy to park your car on the street and see everyone around you roll their eyes in contempt?

Life is going to be hard. You may often find yourself to be cold, sick and unhappy. But you can hold your head up high with dignity because you did something wonderful for which everyone respects you.

WWYR?

Every time that you go out in public, have to wear a sign around your neck that says 'please talk to me'?

OR

Every time that you go out in public, have to wear a sign around your neck that says 'please ignore me'?

Things to Consider

Does unsolicited conversation from strangers annoy you? Or do you crave attention from new people who you don't know?

Are you happy in your own company? Or will this be a terrible social impediment for you? Would you have to tell everyone to ignore the sign? Will people then think that you are confused or crazy?

WWYR?

HIt a homerun in a baseball match in front of a packed stadium?

OR

Make a 147 break on a snooker table while no one is watching?

Things to Consider

Do you want to hear the crowd go wild cheering for what you have done? Lots of homeruns have been hit over the years. Yours will be captured on film and preserved forever more.

A 147 break is a rare thing. Would like to be one of the few people who have ever achieved it? Even if no one else sees it? Would anyone believe you if it wasn't witnessed?

WWYR?

Hit a hole in one whilst playing golf with your friends?

OR

Score the winning goal in the soccer World Cup (the ball simply deflects off you and goes into the net)?

Things to Consider

Most golfers go through their careers without experiencing this pleasure. Your friends will always remember this and you will have an amazing story to tell for the rest of your life.

Do you want the glory of the whole world witnessing you changing history? Do you want the fame even though you will be remembered as the guy who claimed the glory without taking an active part in the goal?

WWYR?

Commit an act of treason which significantly damages the security of your country?

OR

Kidnap one child and hold it hostage for a year?

Things to Consider

Can you cope with morally compromising yourself and letting down every citizen of your country? You will, of course, be very well paid for your duplicitous work.

Instead of affecting everyone in the country you are only hurting one child and its family. Nobody dies and the family are reunited after a year. But will the family be irreparably psychologically damaged?

WWYR?

Be a fly on the wall in Churchill's War Cabinet meetings?

OR

Secretly listen in to what went on in Hitler's Fuhrer bunker?

Things to Consider

Are you fascinated to know about the difficult decisions that were made at the height of the War? This choice brings with it the obvious peril of transforming into a fly which has the associated risk of being swatted by a member of the Cabinet.

Well, you're not a fly which is surely a good thing. But do you really want to be witness to the horrific conversations that must have gone on in these rooms?

WWYR?

Sleep in a morgue overnight with 20 fresh cadavers? **OR** Sleep overnight in an abattoir full of hanging animal carcasses?

Things to Consider

Would you find this interesting and think of it as an opportunity to forever have an amazing anecdote to tell? Or is this experience likely to leave you traumatised?

Would you be able to close your eyes and go to sleep? Are you vegetarian or vegan? If so, is this scenario unbearable to you?

WWYR?

Never feel extreme emotions again?

OR

Only be able to feel extreme emotions all of the time?

Things to Consider

Having no highs and lows would feel stable. But would you miss feeling overjoyed or exhilarated?

This could feel amazing but also awful. Could you cope with continual dramatic swings of emotion?

WWYR?

Have one tooth extracted with pliers, without anaesthetic?

OR

Have all of your fingernails and toenails pulled out with pliers?

Things to Consider

This is going to be excruciating. The reason that this procedure is so painful is that teeth contain nerve endings. At least it's only one tooth being removed. But what if it takes lots of tugs to release it?

Sometimes nails don't grow back and, when they do, regrowth can take up to 18 months. What if only some grow back? Will you look silly? And there's the pain: assuming you're intact, that's 20 agonising moments of extraction.

Printed in Great Britain
by Amazon